a world of Pausabilities

An Exercise in Mindfulness

Written By
Frank J. Sileo, PhD
Illustrated By
Jennifer Zivoin

Magination Press • Washington, DC • American Psychological Association

To my dear friend Sandy. Thank you for introducing me to the world of mindfulness—*FJS*
For Olivia & Elyse, James & Fulton, and Allie & Owen—*JZ*

Published by
MAGINATION PRESS®
An Educational Publishing Foundation Book
American Psychological Association
750 First Street NE
Washington, DC 20002

Magination Press is a registered trademark of the American Psychological Association.

For more information about our books, including a complete catalog, please write to us,
call 1-800-374-2721, or visit our website at www.apa.org/pubs/magination.

Book design by Gwen Grafft
Printed by Lake Book Manufacturing Inc., Melrose Park, IL

Library of Congress Cataloging-in-Publication Data

Names: Sileo, Frank J., 1967- author. | Zivoin, Jennifer, illustrator.
Title: A world of pausabilities : an exercise in mindfulness / by Frank J.
    Sileo ; illustrated by Jennifer Zivoin.
Description: Washington, DC : Magination Press, [2017] | "American
    Psychological Association." | Summary: "Children (and adults) live in a
    fast-paced, demanding and stressful world. It is often difficult to
    slow-down our children's minds and bodies. This book was written to teach
    children to take a pause in their lives, to stop activity, to understand
    quiet time, and to think about what they are doing and where they are
    going"—Provided by publisher.
Identifiers: LCCN 2016012101 | ISBN 9781433823237 (hardcover) |
    ISBN 1433823233 (hardcover)
Subjects: | CYAC: Stories in rhyme. | Mindfulness (Psychology)—Fiction.
Classification: LCC PZ8.3.S58254 Wo 2017 | DDC [E]—dc23 LC record
    available at https://lccn.loc.gov/2016012101

Manufactured in the United States of America
10 9 8 7 6 5 4 3 2 1

Do you know what a PausABiLity is?

A pausability is taking a ***pause*** just for you,
to stop and notice what you feel, think, and do.

A pause is being in the moment
and giving yourself a break.
There's no wrong way to pause
so it's hard to make a mistake.

Some pauses are silent, while some keep you moving.
Pauses should be calming, so things can start improving.

Come let's explore a world of pausabilities!

Take a breath deep from your belly,
and let it out slow.
Relax your muscles until
they feel like dough.

Have something yummy
and healthy to eat.
Notice the flavor;
is it salty, or sweet?

Go outside and take a walk.
Listen to silence; try not to talk.

Let the rays of the sun
warm your body and face.
Take time to slow down,
there's no reason to race.

Draw, paint, color, or just doodle.
Make your body limp like a spaghetti noodle.

Wear your favorite and most comfortable clothes.
Be in the moment and wiggle your toes.

Be good to your body and to your brain.
Take the time to listen to the sound of the rain.

Turn off all things that have a screen.
Splash your face with warm water and make it clean.

See your reflection and make a huge smile.
Smiling makes us feel good and that lasts awhile.

Say something nice to yourself about you.
You are kind, smart, and other things, too!

Reach your arms to the floor and take a bow.
Taking a pause focuses on what's happening now.

Stretch, stretch up as far as you can reach.
Step barefoot in the grass or the sand at the beach.

Notice the wind when it blows through your hair.
Take a pause on your bed, or in a soft chair.

Remember a funny story or a silly joke.
Visit a furry friend and give them a gentle stroke.

Find someone you love and ask for a hug.
Wrap yourself in a blanket so you feel comfy and snug.

Accept what you are feeling as neither right nor wrong.
Taking a pause will make your mind and body strong.

Taking a pause does not have to be hard.
Take a pause in your room, at school, on the bus, or in your yard.

Taking a pause is easy, you see;
making time to pause and practicing is key!

Have you learned how to take a pause?
If so, give yourself a round of applause!

When dealing with
life's difficulties,
stop and think about a
world of pausabilities.

Can you come up with
other pausabilities?
Just let them flow, there are
endless possibilities!

What's in your world of pausabilities?

Note to Parents and Caregivers

In a world of academic, social, occupational, and personal demands, both children and adults are often too busy and moving in too many different directions. As our world becomes more demanding and competitive, even young children often find themselves struggling to balance their many responsibilities and activities with limited time to rest, relax, or take a moment for themselves.

What is Mindfulness?

Mindfulness is bringing your attention to what is happening to you in the present moment. It is not concerned with what happened in the past or what may happen in the future. When you engage in mindfulness, you should do so with a curious, accepting mind without judging what you are feeling or experiencing.

Mindfulness practices have been shown to lower stress, build resilience, and provide clarity in solving problems. They may also have positive effects on anxiety, depression, impulse control, decision-making, learning, memory, and regulating emotions. By nature, children seem to live in the moment better than adults. As adults, we may function in an autopilot mode, thinking about what we have done, should have done, or need to do, without giving much thought or feeling to the moment. Children are often not focused on the past or the future, but rather on what they are doing *right now*—the present moment. However, our world has become increasingly hectic and multi-faceted for children as well as adults, and as a result children find themselves distracted, overwhelmed, and not engaged in that present moment. Children also tend to look for immediate gratification, and teaching mindfulness is a way of slowing down that way of thinking.

What is a Pausability?

Pausability is a whimsical, made-up word that plays on the word *possibility*. In this book, the word *pausability* is used to describe a moment of mindfulness, or the ability to take a pause in our lives. A pause is a mindful exercise that reminds us to be in the present, take a breath, take a break, and pay attention to our feelings, thoughts, sensations, and the world around us. Tuning in to our senses and our breath immediately brings us into the present. Taking a pause also helps children get out of the habit of bouncing between activities and experiences without taking in what is going on for them in the present moment. A pause gives the child more time to think about and make different, perhaps better, choices in their lives.

Some pauses are quiet and calming, like taking a deep breath, turning off electronics, and taking time to slow down. Some are active, such as walking, drawing, painting or doodling, and wiggling your toes. Some involve using your senses, such as learning to listen to the silence or the sound of rain, feeling the sun on your body and face, and feeling the wind blow through your hair. Encourage children to pay attention to details. For example, when they pause to feel the wind blow through their hair, ask them, "Is the air warm or cool?" "Do you smell something in the air, like grass, a flower, or the BBQ next door?"

Learning to Pause

For children, learning how to take a pause requires practice and support from adults, just like learning to play an instrument or ride a bicycle. We want to encourage children to pause so that they can catch their breath; be in the moment; experience what they are thinking, feeling, and doing; and regulate their emotions and behavior.

Know when to pause. Anytime! Initially, however, it's a good idea to introduce pauses when the child is calm. They will be much more focused and compliant, and more likely to be successful. If you try to teach a pause when a child is already upset, they may not be able to properly process what you are trying to teach them. Be aware of the emotional and behavioral triggers in your child. For example, if your child struggles with homework, remind them ahead of time about taking a pause or two. If they start to get upset, help them acknowledge what they are feeling and thinking without judging themselves, and then implement a pause. You could say, "I know that math frustrates you. Math can be a frustrating subject. Let's take a moment, realize you are frustrated, and then we can take a pause by washing our face." Once a child knows how to pause, it will be easier for them to apply it to more emotional situations.

But pauses are not just to be taken when things are not going well for the child—a pause when feeling good helps to appreciate the moment and even to remember it better in the future. If you are at a carnival, encourage your child to pause and take in the smell of the cotton candy, the sounds, and the sensations of the rides.

Know where to pause. Anywhere! Encourage children to think about taking a pause in all situations: not just the home, but during school, extracurricular activities, and even time with friends. Teachers might encourage pauses to start or end their students' day, before a test, or after a stimulating activity such as physical education or recess. Coaches might suggest a pause before or after a game, before going up to bat, or after a missed goal. Caregivers involved in the arts may encourage children to take a pause before, after, or even in the middle of a performance.

Different types of pausing are appropriate for different situations. Help your child to choose a pause that doesn't interfere too much with the task at hand. Taking a long walk or playing with the dog may not be optimal when doing homework. A pause that is more sensory, like a face wash, noticing smells or temperature, or feeling something soft may be more conducive to the quick break they need.

Be patient. Children may initially become frustrated when learning to take a pause. Your patience with them will help them feel more confident about relying on taking a pause when things get difficult. Be aware that children may give up easily or make negative statements like "This is boring!" "Why do I have to do this?" or "I feel silly!" If you child says such things, don't dismiss them. Acknowledge their feelings and tell them that taking pauses might seem strange in the beginning. Focus on the effort made by the child and the positive results from engaging in mindful pausing. The more that a child practices taking pauses, the more comfort and success they will experience. Have them choose a pause that they enjoy or has worked for them before. Your attitude about taking a pause is key to their success as well. Encourage them to practice. Practice together! Pauses are good for everyone!

Acknowledge differences. Some children may have an easier time pausing than others. The pauses you use should be based on your child's age and developmental level. Children with certain clinical issues such as Attention Deficit Hyperactivity Disorder; depression; anxiety; or problems with impulse control, emotional regulation, or executive functioning may have more difficulty slowing down to pause, even while they have a greater need for taking pauses in their daily lives. Learning to successfully pause and be mindful may greatly impact their overall emotional and behavioral functioning.

Children learn from you. Children notice how adults around them deal with frustration, anger, disappointment, and difficulties in their lives, as well as how they express positive emotions like joy, love, contentment, and peace. The manner in which you handle difficult emotions and situations will greatly influence how children will react when met with challenges of their own. Share with your children something that is difficult for you. Let them know that you are taking a pause to get in control and to handle the situation better. You might say, "I am feeling stressed about the traffic today. I am going to take a pause and go for a walk before I make dinner." When you are experiencing a positive emotion or situation, also model taking a pause such as "I had such a great day, I am going to put on my comfy pajamas and snuggle with the dog to really enjoy this feeling."

Endless Pausabilities!

Many pauses have been suggested in this book, but these are not the only possibilities! After reading, foster discussion with your child about other pauses they can try. Encourage them to use their imaginations and creativity. Make it fun and playful—make your child curious about pauses! Start slowly and gradually build on the concept of regularly taking pauses in their lives. Being mindful and engaging in mindfulness is a way of being, not just an activity!

Taking a pause should never replace other treatment modalities such as psychotherapy or medication if needed. If your child continues to struggle emotionally or behaviorally at home, school, or other settings, it may be appropriate to seek a consultation from a licensed psychologist or other licensed mental health professional.

About the Author

Frank J. Sileo, PhD, is a New Jersey licensed psychologist and the founder and executive director of The Center for Psychological Enhancement in Ridgewood, New Jersey. He received his doctorate from Fordham University in New York City. In his practice, Dr. Sileo works with children, adolescents, adults, and families. Since 2010, he has been consistently recognized as one of New Jersey's top kids' doctors. He is the author of five other children's books, *Toilet Paper Flowers: A Story for Children About Crohn's Disease, Hold the Cheese Please: A Story for Children About Lactose Intolerance, Bug Bites and Campfires: A Story for Kids About Homesickness, Sally Sore Loser: A Story About Winning and Losing,* and *Don't Put Yourself Down in Circus Town: A Story About Self-Confidence.* His books *Sally Sore Loser* and *Don't Put Yourself Down in Circus Town* are the Gold Medal recipients of the prestigious Mom's Choice Awards. Dr. Sileo speaks across the country and does author visits. Dr. Sileo has been published in psychological journals and is often quoted in newspapers, magazines, podcasts, webcasts, radio, and television. Learn more about Dr. Sileo on his website, drfranksileo.com.

About the Illustrator

Jennifer Zivoin has always loved art and storytelling, so becoming an illustrator was a natural career path. She has been trained in media ranging from figure drawing to virtual reality, and earned her Bachelor of Arts degree with highest distinction from the honors division of Indiana University. During her professional career, Jennifer worked as a graphic designer and then as a creative director before finding her artistic niche illustrating children's books. When she is not creating art in her studio, her favorite "pausabilities" include drinking cocoa while reading a good book, swimming on hot summer days, and spending time outside with her family. Jennifer lives in Indiana with her husband and two daughters.

About Magination Press

Magination Press is an imprint of the American Psychological Association, the largest scientific and professional organization representing psychologists in the United States and the largest association of psychologists worldwide.